IMAGES
of America

CHIPPEWA LAKE PARK

IMAGES
of America

CHIPPEWA LAKE
PARK

David W. and Diane DeMali Francis

ARCADIA
PUBLISHING

Published by Arcadia Publishing
Charleston, South Carolina

Library of Congress Catalog Card Number: 2004101541

For all general information contact Arcadia Publishing at:
Telephone 843-853-2070
Fax 843-853-0044
E-mail sales@arcadiapublishing.com
For customer service and orders:
Toll-Free 1-888-313-2665

Visit us on the Internet at www.arcadiapublishing.com

CONTENTS

INTRODUCTION

Located on the banks of Ohio's largest natural lake, Chippewa Lake Park never ranked among America's great amusement parks. For one thing, it lacked the quantity and quality of rides that were offered by competitors like Cedar Point, Euclid Beach Park, and Idora Park. Although a popular attraction, Chippewa's roller coaster didn't provide the kind of thrills its larger, more famous cousins did. And Chippewa's beloved carousel wasn't an elaborate product of one of the well-known companies such as Philadelphia Toboggan, William Dentzel, or M.C. Illions.

Furthermore, although it was surrounded by summer cottages, Chippewa was not considered a great summer resort. The park did boast a hotel, but it was rustic at best, with few amenities. Yet, in spite of its modest appearance and facilities, Chippewa Lake Park was destined to become one of Ohio's longest-lived and best-loved amusement parks.

A major reason for the success of Chippewa Lake Park was its location on beautiful Chippewa Lake. Situated in Medina County, Chippewa Lake is a 385-acre body of water, fed by underwater springs and measuring approximately 40 feet at its deepest point. In the earliest days, Native Americans hunted and fished in the Chippewa Valley. Later, in the years preceding the Civil War, local residents used the area for picnics. But it wasn't until a Seville, Ohio, druggist, Edwin Andrews, opened a small summer resort there on July 4, 1875, that Chippewa Lake Park officially became a commercial venture.

Located on a bluff overlooking the lake, Andrews' "Upper Grounds" resort offered dancing, food and beverage services, a small carousel, a hotel, roller coaster, and other entertainments. A decade after Andrews opened his resort, Oscar Townsend and the Cleveland, Lorain, and Wheeling Railroad developed a "Lower Grounds" resort just south of the Andrews property.

Eventually, the Lower Grounds resort became known as Chippewa Lake Park. Around the year 1900, Albert McDowell "Mac" Beach became general manager of the facility, thereby establishing a 70-year relationship between Chippewa Lake Park and the Beach family.

After the First World War, the Chippewa Lake Park Company was formed bringing both the resort and the lake under the same ownership. This event ended a series of long-standing disputes between lake owners and resort operators. Late in 1923, concessionaire Larry Collister received permission from the park owners to begin construction of an amusement midway. He formed the Clean Play Company and granted Mac Beach $2,000 in Clean Play stock in return for managing the midway. Collister also formed other companies to build and market new cottage communities located north and south of the park.

The Great Depression and the abandonment of interurban service delivered a crippling blow to the park. A change in executive management in 1933 did not alleviate financial troubles, and a year later, the park was placed in the hands of a court-appointed receiver. The park was leased to Larry Collister in 1935, but failed to make a profit. The next year it was leased to Mac Beach's son, Parker.

In 1937, Parker Beach managed to purchase both the park and the lake. Under the personal direction of Parker and his wife Janet, Chippewa Lake Park enjoyed a Golden Age that lasted until 1969. Beach ran a safe and clean park that welcomed families and tolerated no misbehavior. With the Big Band Era in full swing, Beach made the ballroom a centerpiece of the park's operation. Even after the Big Band Era ended, Beach continued to fill the ballroom with dancers and famous bands up through the 1969 season.

During the 1960s, Parker Beach began to think about retiring and selling the park. At the conclusion of the 1969 season, Beach sold the park and the lake to Continental Business Enterprises, Incorporated, a Cleveland industrial holding company headed by G.E. DiGeronimo. The new owners added rides, closed the hotel, demolished old buildings, initiated a master development plan and constructed a fence around the park to help improve security and reduce insurance costs. Future plans for Chippewa Lake Park included a year-round resort hotel to be located on the lakeshore just north of the park. Short-sighted opposition from local residents and some government officials caused the cancellation of the project and, in effect, sealed the fate of Chippewa Lake Park.

Attendance at Chippewa Lake Park actually increased during the 1970s, but rising operational costs and high insurance premiums put the park in an untenable financial position. Further, the little park was unable to keep pace with the rapid development of competitors such as Cedar Point and Geauga Lake. Chippewa Lake Park showed a profit of just $28,078 in 1970. The following year it lost an equal amount. The park's last profitable season came in 1974. Two seasons later, the operation lost $90,610. At the end of the 1978 season, the officers of the company met for lunch at the nearby Oaks Lodge (previously a hotel owned by the park) and made the painful decision to close the park.

After more than 100 years of operation, Chippewa Lake Park joined the ghostly ranks of competitors like Euclid Beach, Luna Park, Meyers Lake, Summit Beach, Silver Lake, Puritas Springs, and Crystal Beach. Youngstown's Idora Park held on for a few more seasons, and when it finally closed, the last of Northern Ohio's traditional amusement parks was gone.

We hope the images in this volume will help to keep Chippewa Lake Park alive in your hearts and minds. If you once visited Chippewa Lake, we hope these images will take you back to lazy, carefree days by the lake. And if you never had a chance to walk the midway at Chipp, perhaps this book will help you understand why Chippewa Lake Park held a cherished spot in the hearts of your parents and grandparents.

One

The Emergence of an Amusement Park

During the pre-amusement park era, Chippewa offered simple resort facilities that included dancing, picnicking, band concerts, games, and lake excursions on small steamboats.

Hotel Chippewa welcomed its first guests during the 1880s and remained a centerpiece of the park for almost 100 years. Last used as a hotel in 1969, it housed park offices and storage facilities until the park closed in 1978. Below the hotel were the freezers and coolers for the park's restaurant and food stands.

An inlet and an outlet at the north and south ends of Chippewa Lake help maintain water levels and provide picturesque beauty spots. The park used a dam on the outlet to keep water levels high in summer and to lower the levels in fall before the lake froze.

10

In summer, a thick growth of water lilies appeared at both ends of Chippewa Lake. These patches of lily pads have always been a favorite spot for fishing.

A pre-1920 view of the park shows the pier, the first bathhouse, a refreshment stand, and a carousel building. The building in front of the pier eventually became the restaurant and part of the main pavilion.

A pier for steamboat docking and rowboat rental was constructed during the park's early years. Around 1910, this wooden pier featured a small canvas awning to shield waiting steamboat passengers from the summer sun.

Ready for a Morning Ride,   Chippewa Lake, Ohio.

Although a passenger boat may have operated on Chippewa Lake as early as 1854, documented evidence says passenger pleasure craft sailed the lake from 1875 to 1978. Gasoline-powered and equipped with a searchlight for nighttime use, *Skip* was a popular launch in service before World War I.

12

During the early 1900s, the Community Club Company constructed the Community Club Hotel just north of the park. The hotel later became Tarry Tavern and made newspaper headlines when a murder was committed there.

The Bowling Alley and Pool building later became the park's skating rink. In front of the building are the station and tracks of the Cleveland and Southwestern interurban line, whose fast green electric cars brought thousands of visitors to Chippewa.

Chippewa Lake Park

THE LARGEST AND MOST BEAUTIFUL LAKE AND PARK IN OHIO.

Chippewa Lake Park Co.,

Chippewa Lake, O.

A. M. Beach, Manager.

W. H. LANPHEAR, JR., Cleveland Representative.

An early park brochure reveals that a room at Hotel Chippewa cost $2 a day or $10 a week. A furnished cottage rented for $10 a week, and a large, furnished tent cost just $5 a week. Camping sites, gasoline stoves, and mattresses were also available.

Rowboats that could be rented from the park at 25¢ per hour shared the pleasures of Chippewa Lake with privately owned gasoline or naphtha launches. A few small steam launches and numerous sailboats added to the congestion on weekends.

Around 1918, a sailboat passes the Townsend estate north of the park. The park company acquired the Townsend property and converted the home to the Oaks Hotel. Later, this property became the Oaks Lodge restaurant.

Chippewa's first bathhouse was little more than a frame cottage with changing rooms for swimmers. Before 1920, visitors were permitted to drive cars into the facility and park in the shade of the trees.

At the time of the First World War, the lake shore was dotted with a series of small refreshment stands and game concessions. A seaplane circle swing ride (seen behind the parked cars) operated near the beach.

16

Across from Hotel Chippewa was the park's dancing pavilion. Although adequate in 1910, the pavilion proved too small to handle increasing dance crowds after the First World War.

The park's newspaper advertising for July 4, 1922, touted new rides, new facilities, dancing to Rosenthal's Orchestra, and free performances by aerial acrobat George T. Wright.

Among the improvements for the 1922 season was a new carousel from the Allan Herschell Company of North Tonawanda, New York. Herschell was America's most prolific carousel builder, producing more than 3,000 machines.

Also new for the 1922 season was a circle swing ride from the R.S. Uzzell Company The ride simulated flight, and passengers enjoyed a breezy adventure in cars designed to look like biplanes.

An early 1920s view from the west side of the hill where Hotel Chippewa, the dancing pavilion, and Refreshment Stand "A" were situated. Until its last year of operation, Chippewa's grounds were mostly tree shaded.

The final season for the old bathhouse (extreme left) was 1921. In the distance is a refreshment stand, rental rowboats, and a pavilion.

The new bathhouse debuted in the spring of 1922. It featured small changing rooms, a check room, a sales counter for beach novelties, and employee dormitories on the second floor.

Among the aesthetic improvements of the early 1920s were pristine white lamp posts and lattice-work arches. The lamp posts on the pier survived until the park closed in 1978.

The Chippewa Lake Park Company replaced the aging wooden dock with a substantial concrete pier. The "L" shaped pier created a protective slip where rowboats, launches, and speedboats were shielded from storms and west winds.

Miss Chippewa was originally one of a fleet of boats built for service at Akron's Summit Beach Park. She was later transported to Chippewa where she served for 50 seasons.

The company's largest investment was the massive picnic pavilion with its magnificent view of the lake. The building housed the restaurant, Refreshment Stand "B", a rifle range, souvenir stand, games, and picnic tables that accommodated more than 1,000 people. Employee dormitories were located on the second floor.

Descending the hill from Hotel Chippewa and the dancing pavilion, visitors came upon an entranceway that welcomed them to the new Funland midway.

Milo E. Huth, an arcade machine manufacturer and major shareholder in the Chippewa Lake Park Company, built a new Penny Arcade in 1923. Two years earlier, Huth had erected a smaller arcade and funhouse near the beach.

At the close of the 1922 season, the old dancing pavilion was razed, and a cavernous new ballroom rose on its site. The new ballroom featured a huge dance floor, ample seating, and a refreshment bar.

Under the new ballroom was space for a grocery store, restrooms, and a workshop that later became the Chippewa Boat Works. Stand "A" (left) stayed open late to serve food and beverages to dancers.

The new ballroom hosted Johnson's Society Orchestra, Rosenthal's Orchestra, and the dance bands of Carter Ginis, Emerson Gill, Austin Wylie, George Williams, and Jimmy Dimmick. Later, Lawrence Welk's Orchestra spent an entire summer in the ballroom.

24

Chippewa's only major roller coaster was designed by John A. Miller in 1924. Miller was commissioned by Fred Pearce of Detroit, whose company owned roller coasters as well as entire parks including Walled Lake and Jefferson Beach in Michigan.

On a sunny day during August of 1924, riders took the first plunge on Chippewa's new coaster. The ride cost Pearce $53,000 to construct and remained part of the Pearce amusement empire through the 1969 season.

The station of the new coaster was typical of coaster installations of the 1920s. The man in the foreground operated the brake levers, while the other man collected fares for re-rides. At the left is a spare train on the storage track.

The station of the new Big Dipper roller coaster was strategically located on the southeast corner of the midway. In 1925, a ride on the coaster cost 15¢, but a re-ride was just 10¢.

The Merry Mix-Up was a simple circle swing ride with chairs suspended from cables that swung out from the tower as the ride turned with increasing speed. Behind the ride is the new main picnic pavilion.

At the center of the new midway, where Kiddieland would later stand, was the Auto Speedway. The Speedway featured Custer Cars, among the industry's first driver-controlled race cars. They were invented by L.L. Custer and built at the Custer Specialty Company in Dayton.

The station of the Scenic Shore Railroad featured lattice-work that was a design hallmark of Chippewa's new midway. Games were later built on the site of the miniature railroad station.

The locomotive and passenger cars of the Scenic Shore Railroad were built by the Cagney Brothers of New York. Best known for their attractive miniature steam engines, the Cagney Brothers also built a small number of clumsy, unattractive gasoline engines like the one at Chippewa.

28

The midway's Pony Track offered children rides on ponies of all sizes. Those unwilling to mount a saddle could opt for a pony cart ride. Each pony wore a circus-style feather plume on its head.

While the Pony Track catered to children, the Pony Hotel rented saddle horses to adults. The three riders were cottage renters during the late 1920s.

On a hot summer afternoon, visitors gathered across from Hotel Chippewa to enjoy a concert. The area where the stage was situated later became the miniature golf course.

This photo, taken about 1925, shows the ballroom (left), Refreshment Stand "A" (center), and the back of another refreshment stand that later was moved to the picnic grove. Note the shoe shine stand on the porch of Hotel Chippewa at the extreme right.

A Cleveland photographer captured this view of the parking lot at capacity during the mid-1920s. In the foreground are the tracks of the Cleveland and Southwestern interurban railway.

It was a long and dusty walk from the center of the parking lot to the midway, the hotel, or the ballroom. The building at the edge of the parking lot housed the bowling alleys and pool tables.

Refreshment Stand "A", located across from Hotel Chippewa, always featured picturesque landscaping on its eastern lawn. It also offered an outdoor dining terrace that was especially popular with the ballroom crowd.

Perhaps ready for a dance, a beautifully attired young lady poses in front of the landscaping below Stand "A."

The stand on the corner of the pavilion, which would later be known as Stand "E," was originally used to promote real estate development in the cottage communities of Gloria Glens and Briarwood Beach. A lot in the latter village could be purchased for $245 during the mid-1920s.

Anticipating an interest in night bathing, a line of lamp posts were placed across the beach and searchlights were mounted on the bathhouse. Thanks in part to cool evenings and the lure of the midway and the ballroom, nocturnal bathing never became a popular pastime.

Swimming on hot summer afternoons made Chippewa Lake a popular summer retreat. At times, however, there seemed to be more spectators than bathers.

On a late morning during the summer of 1928, children enjoy the swings on the beach. At the pier, *Miss Chippewa* and a small launch, probably *Bertha*, await the day's activity.

34

A number of ice houses operated on park grounds and harvested ice from the lake during winter. During the late 1920s, an interurban car demolished one of the ice delivery trucks, killing the driver.

In 1921, ex-army pilot Captain Philip Goembel established a flying field on the west side of the lake. Goembel and his brother John gave flying lessons in surplus "Jennys," offered passenger rides, and operated a boat between the park and the little airport.

Tarry Tavern, formerly the Community Club Hotel, became a trendy vacation spot during the 1920s. In addition to fine food and water sports, the hotel offered guests an excellent tennis court.

Tarry Tavern was at the zenith of its popularity during the 1920s when it was necessary to make reservations in early spring to be assured a room during the summer. In 1924, 9,000 people stayed at the hotel, many from Cleveland and Akron.

In 1924, 600,000 people visited Chippewa Lake Park and a season later Larry Collister claimed that 1,000,000 had strolled the midway. The largest single day was July 4, 1924, when an estimated 47,000 people came to Chippewa. By 1926, the Clean Play Company claimed a midway income of $170,000.

While 47,000 people packed the midway, the cottage areas north of the park were peaceful, restful, and picturesque. Small piers accommodated private rowboats, sailboats, and launches.

The pier at Tarry Tavern was reserved exclusively for the use of hotel guests and the hostelry maintained a small fleet of rental row boats.

The beaches at Briarwood Beach and Chippewa-on-the-Lake were open to cottage owners and renters only. Unlike the park beach, they were rarely crowded or noisy.

Chippewa's bathing beauties of the 1920s were permitted to wear more revealing swim suits than were there mothers of a decade earlier. Still, woolen suits became unpleasantly heavy when wet and dried slowly.

Typical cottages of the 1920s had a small second floor for bedrooms, a screened porch, and plenty of windows for ventilation. Many had no interior walls and rooms were created with partitions that did not reach the ceiling.

Most cottages were personalized with names such as Twin Oaks, Idlewild, Chat-a-While, or Lakewood. While one side of Lakewood cottage fronted on a dusty lane, the other side offered magnificent views of vibrant sunsets over Chippewa Lake.

Most of Chippewa's cottages were furnished with older cast off furniture, lamps, mattresses, and dinnerware. Nevertheless, the cottages were always comfortable and cozy.

Two

DEPRESSION, WAR, AND SURVIVAL

The late 1920s and the 1930s were not kind to the amusement park industry. Even before the Depression, parks were struggling. Cleveland's Luna Park closed in 1929, and Akron's Riverview Park was shuttered a year later. Chippewa survived the trauma of thinning crowds and decreased spending, but not without some harrowing financial experiences.

On this beautiful summer evening during the 1930s, the midway at Chippewa was almost empty. The Zombie, next to the Arcade, was a walk-though funhouse. Beyond the funhouse was the Dashing Dodgems ride.

After a major summer storm, the lake level rose and submerged the park's pier. *Miss Chippewa* continued to operate by taking on passengers at an open gate of the main pavilion.

A portion of the parking lot was converted into a midget auto racing track, enticing drivers to visit Chippewa from all over the region.

The midget race cars were fast, noisy, and dangerous. In this photo, smoke pours from a damaged car that has crashed over the safety rail.

At the end of every season, the park was winterized and rides were partially disassembled and stored. Lamp globes were removed, the tops of lamp post were covered with tar paper, and shutters were fixed on the fronts of games and food stands.

To reduce the danger of ice damage, the water level was lowered in autumn by using a dam at the south end of the lake. In spring, after the ice melted, the dam boards were re-installed, and the water level rose.

During the 1930s and 1940s, the park was open for ice skating when the lake was adequately frozen. When a red and white flag was raised over the pier, skaters and even their dogs gathered on segments of ice prepared for skating.

Each winter when the skating facility opened, the Marine Dining Room became the park's Winter Sports Club. Customers paid 10¢ to skate and could refresh themselves with hot beverages and food in the club house.

In January and February, a few daring adventurers participated in the fast and sometimes dangerous sport of ice boat racing. Ice boats handled much like sailboats but faced the hazard of crashing through thin ice.

Those who thought ice boats were too slow could add an aircraft engine and propeller for increased levels of speed and danger. Parker Beach claimed that *Miss Chippewa* attained speeds in excess of 60 miles per hour on the frozen lake.

The Akron tire companies and their unions were among Chippewa's best customers for summer picnics. During one Goodyear picnic, the blimp *Vigilant* made low passes over the park and the lake.

Albert Chatfield operated the photo studio at Cleveland's Luna Park until that park closed in 1929. He moved to Chippewa Lake in 1930 where he operated the park's photo studio and documented much of the area's history during the Depression.

The picnic grove camp grounds offered low-cost vacations during the 1930s and 1940s. Both tents and trailers were welcome, and a small store sold ice, beverages, and supplies.

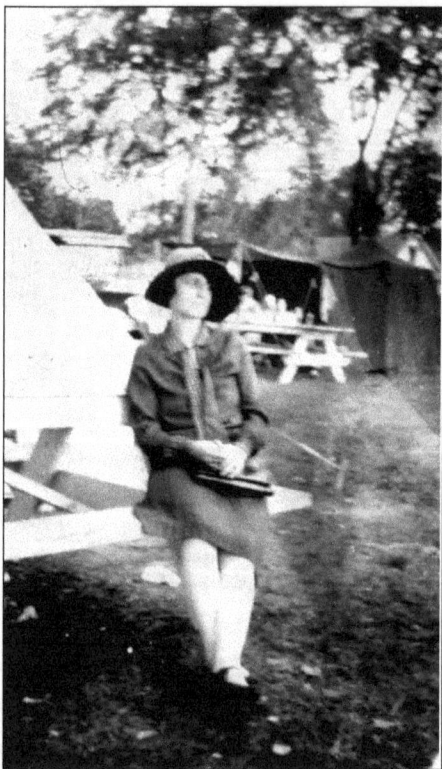

Jessie Hammerstrom, an annual visitor from Cleveland, dressed rather formally while staying with her children in the campgrounds *circa* 1935. During most seasons, she preferred to rent a cottage for a week.

One of the favorite dance bands of the early 1930s was Emerson Gill and his orchestra. Gill had been a featured band at both Chippewa and at Cleveland's Luna Park during the 1920s.

The interior of Chipp's ballroom was redecorated during the 1930s. The 1920s chandeliers were removed, new lights and a crystal ball were installed, and the stage was redecorated.

At various times, the ballroom was called the Starlight Ballroom, and the redecorated stage justified the name.

Over the years, the ballroom was used for numerous events besides dancing. During the 1930s, marksmen in buckskin costumes competed in black powder rifle shooting events.

Under Parker Beach's direction, a sportsman's show was established in the ballroom. Companies displayed canoes, sailboats, outboard engines, midget race cars, and new automobiles.

For more than 50 years, Chippewa's ballroom was the site of numerous beauty pageants. The last beauty pageants, operated by Syd Friedman's All Star Theatrical Agency, were held in 1978.

During a July night in 1940, a bomb was detonated beneath the ballroom. The explosion wrecked a large section of the floor and did major damage to the boat works, restrooms, grocery store, and barber shop.

In 1905, Mac Beach brought his month-old son to Chippewa. Thirty-two years later, Parker Beach (right) purchased the park out of bankruptcy. Along with his wife Janet, Parker successfully managed the park until 1969.

Hotel Chippewa was the center of park activities. In addition to hotel rooms, the old building housed the park offices, cottage rental office, two apartments, the food service office, and coolers and freezers for the restaurant and food stands.

In 1936, the park loaned the speedboat *Dynamite* to the State of Ohio to be used in rescue operations in flood-ravaged Southern Ohio. Park employees sometimes referred to *Dynamite* as "the White Elelphant."

Chippewa was famous for its speedboats for nearly 50 years. In this 1940s view, a speedboat leaves the pier while *Miss Chippewa* loads passengers for the next lake cruise.

By the late 1930s, the beach was equipped with umbrella-covered benches. Next to the beach, a frosted fruit drink stand catered to parched sunbathers.

The midway changed a great deal during the Depression years. Kiddieland was situated south of the main midway, and the Devil's Paradise, a dark ride, was opened just west of the roller coaster station.

A unique children's ride was the Zeppelin Swing. Cars were suspended below metal dirigibles that swung outward as the ride revolved slowly.

55

The Shooting Gallery, adorned with an unauthorized image of Donald Duck with bow and arrow, used live ammunition until the 1960s when compressed air guns made their appearance. Earlier, there had been a Shooting Gallery in the main pavilion.

The Stratoship (right), a ride developed by the R.E. Chambers Company during the mid-1930s, appeared on the midway before World War II. Unfortunately, the Stratoship had limited capacity and failed to deliver much in the way of thrills.

When the Tumble Bug ride was installed, the Airplane Swing was moved to a lakeside location where the Merry Mix-Up had previously operated. Later converted to the Rocket Ship ride, the Airplane Swings remained at this location until 1978.

Industrial picnics were truly the life's blood of Chippewa Lake Park. During a Timken Company picnic from Canton, thousands of boxes of Cracker Jack were distributed to attendees. Other picnics provided complete meals or lemonade, orangeade, and ice cream.

The Kentucky Derby game was an exciting device that allowed players to control the speed of racing metal horses with large wheels. However, if the wheels were spun too fast, the horses slowed down, which challenged players to find just the perfect speed.

The line of buildings in the shadow of the roller coaster's largest hill included the Fish Pond game, a nickel pitch, a gift shop, and a refreshment stand.

When it was constructed, Chippewa's carousel operated under a temporary canvas roof. After a few seasons, a permanent carousel building was constructed to protect the ride. The park's photo studio, originally operated by Bert Chatfield, was located between the carousel and the Arcade.

The Tumble Bug ride, a product of the Traver Engineering Company, was always among the midway's most popular attractions. A rugged, well-built ride, the Tumble Bug lasted from the 1920s to 1978.

Just south of the carousel, the park constructed the games field and an open air stage. Used by group picnics for games and drawings, the stage hosted band concerts, free acts, and beauty pageants.

Here, the tree-shaded midway is viewed from Hotel Chippewa. Tired, thirsty visitors could rest their feet on the many midway benches while enjoying a cool drink purchased at the nearby lemonade stand. To the right is the main pavilion with game stands in front of the picnic table area.

A lake cruise on the *Miss Chippewa* affords a good view of the main pavilion and midway. The Ferris Wheel was later turned 90 degrees in order to reduce the risk of damage from storms and west winds.

Located across from Hotel Chippewa, Stand "A" was the park's largest refreshment stand and one of just two stands that sold beer. The right front corner of Stand "A" housed a small popcorn counter.

When the Y-Flyer sailboat design became popular, the Chippewa Boat Works was established below the ballroom to construct the little boats. Dozens of Y-Flyers, most belonging to Chippewa Lake Yacht Club members, sailed the lake.

During the war years, the old Townsend estate was leased to Helen and Manuel Fraga. The building became the Five Oaks Hotel, offering guest rooms and a restaurant with fabulous views of the lake.

Three

THE POST WAR BOOM

The end of World War II and the start of the Baby Boom brought new prosperity to Chippewa Lake Park. Large crowds, mostly absent during the 1930s, returned to the park, and Chipp entered its Golden Age.

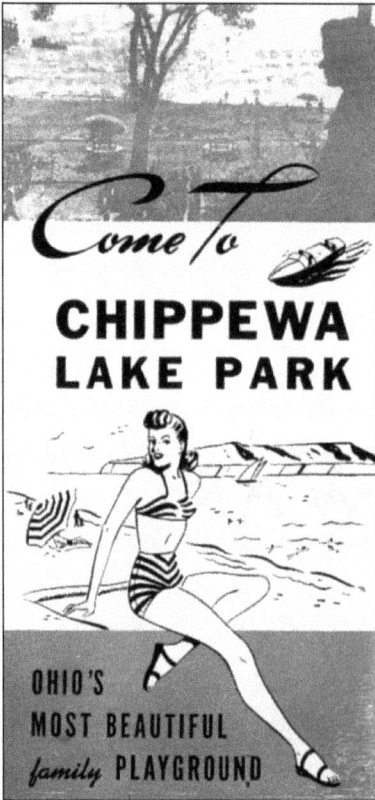

For the first time in years, a new brochure was produced and distributed to promote the park. As always, Parker Beach touted the resort facilities and the lake rather than just the amusement park.

Since virtually every family owned an automobile in post-war America, Chippewa purchased billboard advertising to take advantage of crowded highways. By this time, the Indian chief was the well-known symbol of the park.

The men who directed the park in the postwar era included (left to right), Phil Jacobs (games manager), Parker Beach (general manager), Fred Beach (office and financial manager), and Ace Brigode (group sales, promotions, and ballroom manager).

Ace Brigode (left) was a well-respected dance band leader and former manager of the ballroom at Hiawatha Park in Mount Vernon, Ohio. Tired of traveling with a band, he came to Chippewa to handle the park's sales, promotion, and ballroom duties.

Some amusement parks began adding Kiddielands during the mid-1920s, but the postwar Baby Boom ensured the installation of miniature rides at virtually every park. Chippewa's Kiddieland was located in the center of the main midway, where it remained until the 1970s.

The Pony Cart ride was always a big hit with children because of its cute metal horses and comfortable wooden carts with upholstered seats.

Chippewa's Kiddieland carousel sported whimsical wooden animals including a rabbit, a duck, and a frog. The ride was replaced with a newer model during the early 1970s.

The Flying Saucer ride was added to Kiddieland during the early 1950s. Next to the Flying Saucer was a Mangels Kiddie Whip, the miniaturized version of a popular large midway ride.

A new miniature train, suitable for both adults and children, replaced the old 1920s engine. The Chippewa miniature railroad traveled from the midway to the edge of the parking lot on Lake Road and then back to the midway.

Chippewa's 1922 Allan Herschell Company carousel was always the most popular ride with younger children as well as many adults. During the 1950s, all horses were painted white, but the scenery panels were the original oil paintings by Zelhaus Kahn.

During the Big Band Era, the ballroom went through its final remodeling. New ceiling curtains improved acoustics, and the stage was painted a sparkling white. The name "Chippewa" was spelled out in glittering letters on the stage's proscenium and new red, white, and blue lights were installed over the stage.

The ballroom hosted a number of sportsman's shows after the war, but these events were soon suspended. During the 1970s, an antique show and several other events were held in the ballroom.

During television's early years, amusement parks were used to promote TV shows and the sale of TV sets. One *TV Guide* promotion featured free rides and drawings for television sets and other prizes.

On August 18, 1954, television's popular Annie Oakley (Gail Davis) and Sheriff Lofty Craig (Brad Johnson) appeared at Chippewa. Also on the program were Cleveland television personalities Cousin Kay and Uncle Jake (Gene Carroll).

70

The park utilized a surplus World War II DUKW to promote coming events. The amphibious "Duck" was used in the park and on the lake and also served as a utility vehicle until about 1960.

Parker Beach maintained close ties with a number of Ohio governors. As a result, the park was selected for the Northeastern Ohio Department of State Exposition, August 4–6 of 1948. Governor Thomas Herbert attended the event and delivered a speech in the ballroom.

Although Parker Beach had many political connections, Ace Brigode (left) was the park's promotional genius. Respected and admired by everyone, Brigode promoted the park tirelessly and initiated the publication of a newsletter, *Chippewa Lake Park News*.

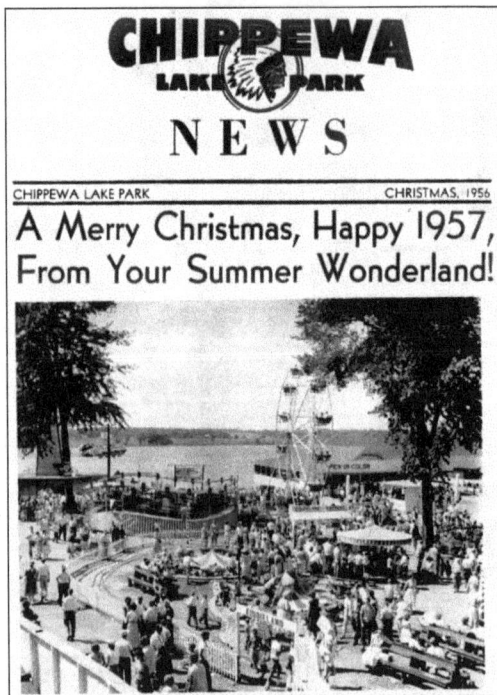

CHIPPEWA
LAKE PARK
N E W S

CHIPPEWA LAKE PARK   CHRISTMAS, 1956

A Merry Christmas, Happy 1957, From Your Summer Wonderland!

The Christmas, 1956 edition of Brigode's *News* included announcements regarding new attractions and events for the 1957 season. Ace's own column, "Breezing With Brigode," featured friendly gossip about how park employees and concessionaires were spending the off-season.

Mistakenly using 1878 as the date of its founding, Chippewa celebrated its 75th birthday in 1953. Despite the error, the season-long birthday party proved successful and the Seville *Chronicle* released a special edition focusing on the park's history.

An amusement park proved the ideal location for almost any kind of outdoor event. Using a portion of the parking lot, the Buckeye Horse Pullers selected Chippewa for one of their contests during the early 1950s.

Railroads spurred the growth of Chippewa before 1920. A few decades later, however, the Baltimore and Ohio Railroad Veterans Association was one of the few outings to travel to the park by train. In 1965, Chippewa welcomed its last railroad excursion.

Larry LeMoyne, a full-blooded Native American, owned the Archery Range located near the roller coaster. After he was killed in an automobile accident, the concession was operated by his wife, Rose.

The beach of the early 1950s featured new ping-pong tables and a small refreshment stand that served cold drinks and snacks. A volleyball net was added during the busy postwar years.

A group of park employees join the bathing beauties as they sunbathe on the lifeguard boat. The park recruited seasonal employees at Ohio colleges, especially Ohio University and Miami University.

Dynamite III was a powerful HackerCraft speedboat that was purchased by Parker Beach during the early 1950s. In this view, the big boat was piloted by Al Tanner, longtime pier manager and educator from Oxford, Ohio.

The Putt Putt boats were owned and operated by concessionaires Helen and Frank Bajcsi. The Bajcsis, who remained at the park through 1969, also owned the Tilt-A-Whirl and the miniature train, the Chippewa Choo Choo.

Especially on weekends, the main pavilion was usually filled to capacity with picnickers. In the background is Refreshment Stand "B," which sold cold drinks, beer, hot dogs, ice cream bars, potato chips, pretzels, coffee, gum, candy, and cigars.

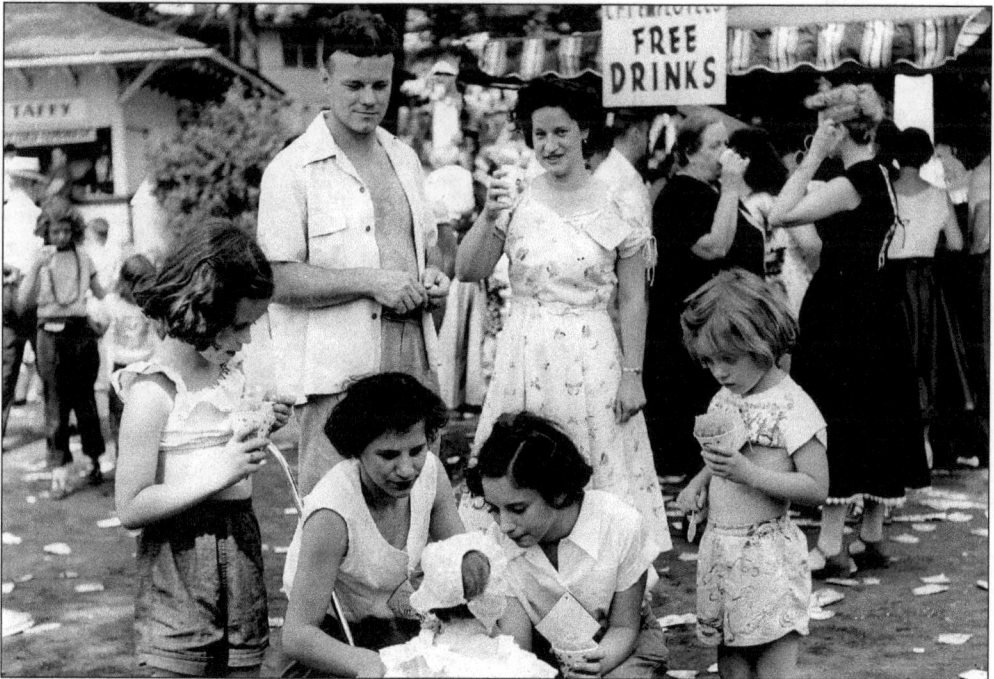

During the Cleveland Pneumatic Tool Company picnic, the park set up a number of portable canvas stands to serve orangeade and loganberry drinks to the employees and their families. The park mixed the beverages in the backroom of Stand "B" and sold them to picnic groups by the gallon.

Foodservice employees in the orangeade stands and throughout the park were required to wear clean, white T-shirts and aprons. Twice a week, female employees were provided with starched white uniform dresses.

The venerable Tumble Bug ride thrilled park visitors from the 1920s to 1978 and was still standing years after the park closed. The maintenance department always kept a spare motor on hand, for the big ride burned out a motor every few years.

Located next to Charles "Dinny" Huth's Arcade was Russ Reynolds' Photo Studio. Reynolds, a school teacher, also operated the Cotton Candy concession until the park closed in 1978.

Parker Beach insisted on immaculate landscaping and employed a gardener during the spring and summer months. A well manicured lawn and neatly trimmed hedge rows led to the U-Drive 'Em boats and the Rocket Ship ride.

The Flying Scooter ride (left) was added to the midway in 1954, as was the Tilt-A-Whirl. Next to the Flying Scooters is the Caterpillar, a fast, covered ride invented by Hyla F. Maynes. The Caterpillar was a mainstay in most parks before 1960.

Chattanooga showman Hal Wilson owned the Ferris Wheel, located between the Tumble Bug and the Rocket Ship ride. For two decades, the Ferris Wheel was advertised as the fastest ride of its kind in the world.

Maintenance is a never-ending task at amusement parks. After the close of the season, Chippewa's crew worked on the Ferris Wheel with the help of the winch truck and the amphibious "Duck."

With a full parking lot in the background, park visitors climb the hill that passes the ballroom as they walk toward Hotel Chippewa and Stand "A." The windows on the lower level of the ballroom look in on the park's grocery store.

After the war, concessionaire Beryl Freudiger prepared the Rocket Ship tower for a sheathing of shiny aluminum that would reflect sunshine by day and spotlights by night. Housing the electric motor that turned the Rockets, the ride's base was also used for lumber storage.

The old Airplane Swing was converted into the Rocket Ship ride by installing stainless steel rocket cars built by the R.E. Chambers Company of Beaver Falls, Pennsylvania.

Fred Pearce, owner of the roller coaster, paid Phil Harper to maintain and oversee the ride's operation. Harper, the park's superintendent, lived in a cottage adjacent to the coaster. His father, Lee, was a member of the coaster's original construction crew.

A repeat ride on the coaster was 20¢ during the 1950s. The line of lights above the "Repeat Ride" sign indicated the number of riders on the train who were paying for a second ride. In this case, the indicator light read "0," reporting no repeat riders.

From the day it opened until the park closed in 1978, the roller coaster was the park's most popular ride (followed by the Dodgem). The building at the lower left is part of the coaster tunnel that led to the lift hill. The other structures are games buildings.

During the post-war years, new Dodgem cars replaced the old 1920s cars. Although the Dodgem was second only to the coaster in popularity, the cars required constant maintenance, and the ride's metal floor required special care during the winter months.

A simulated flight ride, the Fly-O-Plane was one of a number of devices built by the Eyerly Aircraft Company. Seen here behind the Caterpillar, the Fly-O-Plane had limited rider capacity. It was not a profitable ride for Chippewa and lasted only a few seasons.

The Flying Scooter ride, built by the Bisch-Rocco Company of Chicago, was more successful. It enabled riders to experience the sensation of flight. By turning the forward vertical wing themselves, riders could cause the cars to rise and dip.

The Open Air Stage was the scene of most organized events during group outings. In this view, workers at the Cleveland Pneumatic Tool Company picnic distribute thousands of popcorn balls to the children.

Four

CHIPPEWA LAKE PARK
AT ITS ZENITH

Chippewa Lake Park was at its zenith from the late 1950s until Parker Beach sold the park after the 1969 season. During these years, neither Cedar Point nor Geauga Lake posed a great threat to Chippewa, and the operation remained profitable.

Primarily responsible for Chippewa's success during the 1960s was Hank Clark (second from left). Clark was a Chippewa native who studied under Ace Brigode and took over after Brigode's death. He single-handedly booked picnics, placed advertising, conceived promotions, managed the ballroom, ran the restaurant, supervised catering, and operated the midway food services.

Hank Clark hired bands that appealed to teenagers, and as a result, brought huge crowds to the park. At the same time, he retained the tradition of featuring major Big Bands in the ballroom.

Clark's greatest accomplishment was initiating WHLO Appreciation Day on the first Saturday in May. The Akron rock music radio station presented major bands and distributed thousands of records and other prizes.

WHLO Appreciation Day was the biggest event of the season at Chippewa. Although the park claimed an attendance of 60,000, the installation of turnstiles in 1970 showed that actual attendance was somewhat lower at 25,000.

On January 26, 1961, the park's maintenance crew labored to remove large trees that were felled by heavy snows. The brick entrance to the park was replaced a few years later with an illuminated sign.

Some of the maintenance and grounds crew posed in front of the maintenance shop during the summer of 1958. Standing on the right is Bob Foster, longtime grounds manager and dedicated "Chippewa Indian."

"Closed for the Season," read the sign placed near the main entrance to the park each fall. After the rides were disassembled and the park buildings winterized, the maintenance crew began repairing and painting rides for the next season.

In September, *Miss Chippewa* was positioned on her marine railway and pulled out of the water. In spring, her planking had to be caulked with oakum before she could be launched for the season.

After tables and chairs were stacked, the restaurant was converted into a warehouse for the winter. The carousel horses were carefully placed on large sheets of paper to protect their paint from damage.

By the 1950s, the old camp grounds had been converted to "Trailer City." Some residents, including games concessionaire Phil Jacobs, sometimes lived in the trailer park year around.

Next to Trailer City, and eventually absorbing the trailer park, was Chippewa's picnic grove. On weekends, as many as 800 cars jammed the grove. The Picnic Grove Stand sold beverages, charcoal, and picnic supplies to visitors.

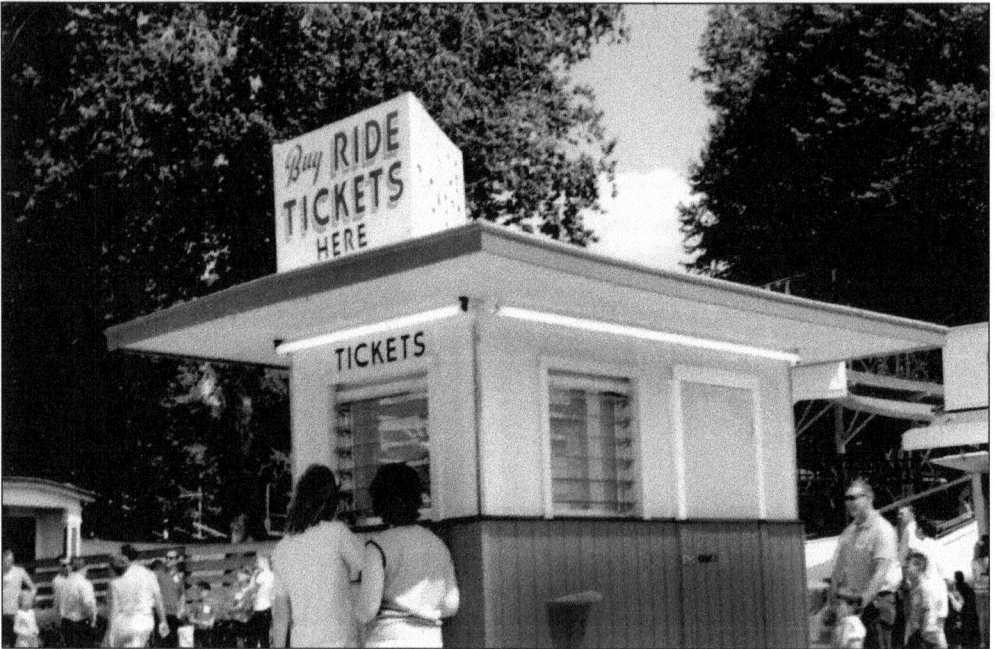

Among Parker Beach's improvements during the early 1960s were three new ticket booths. Every ride required a specified number of 5¢ tickets (except on Tuesday nights, when a Pay-One-Price ticket purchased unlimited rides until closing).

Parker Beach (right) poses with some of the Medina County Sheriff's Deputies who served as the park's police department. Willie Davis (second from left) served as Chippewa's Chief of Security during the 1970s.

The miniature golf course that was constructed near the ballroom stayed open late to accommodate dancers and hotel guests. The house in the background was the residence of Fred Beach, who managed the park's office and owned Scare, the funhouse.

Amusement park owners and managers work long hours during the busy summer months. Late in the evening, Parker Beach's Chrysler and Janet Beach's Thunderbird are still parked near the owner's hotel offices. The door on the left led to Hank Clark's apartment.

After a number of seasons at Cleveland's Puritas Springs Park, Lawrence "Jungle Larry" Tetzlaff moved his Circus Africa to Chippewa in 1959. He and his wife, Safari Jane, exhibited lions, snakes, alligators, African lion dogs, and other animals. They also presented exciting animal shows.

Jungle Larry's Circus Africa was housed in the old skating rink building (left) and remained at Chippewa from 1959 to 1964. In 1965, he moved to Cedar Point and later opened another facility in Naples, Florida.

Stand "A" remained the park's largest and most profitable refreshment stand throughout the 1960s. Below the stand was located the food service warehouse and a large cooler for storing kegs of beer and apples used to make candy apples.

Hotel Chippewa changed very little between the 1920s and the 1960s. Its most pleasant feature was a broad veranda overlooking the lake. With its famous rocking chairs, the veranda provided a perfect view of Chippewa Lake's magnificent sunsets.

The upper row of windows in Hotel Chippewa's south wing brought light into the park offices. The first and second floors held sparsely furnished hotel rooms that served for decades without modernization.

Hot, steamy summers brought hundreds to Chippewa's beach on weekdays, while weekends saw the beach filled to capacity. Since the park restaurant was closed from two to five each afternoon, most waitresses spent the afternoon on the beach.

When heavy rains flooded most of the beach, bathers still came to enjoy the small portion of beach that was not submerged. The umbrellas in the water mark an area that was normally dry sand.

Occasionally, the pier crew also had to cope with flood waters. In order to maintain operations, a temporary pier was constructed to serve *Miss Chippewa* and the speedboats *Dynamite* and *Firecracker*.

By the late 1960s, the venerable *Miss Chippewa* was almost 50 years old. Despite her age, the launch was highly dependable and very stable even on rough water and in high winds.

A photo taken from the first hill of the roller coaster shows Chippewa's main midway as it appeared during the mid-1960s. The walkway on the right led to Hotel Chippewa, the ballroom, Stand "A," and miniature golf.

When Vermilion's Crystal Beach Park closed in 1962, its train was sold and moved to Chippewa. Behind the Chippewa Choo Choo is the Flying Cages ride, another 1960s addition to the park.

Around 1960, Parker Beach began replacing old 1920s wooden fences and lamp posts with more durable chain link fences and steel light poles. In the process, Chippewa lost some of its quaint charm.

The owners of Ponchartrain Beach Park in New Orleans developed "talking" trash collectors in animal shapes that asked children to pick up trash and deposit it in the animal's mouth. Chippewa purchased both Porky the Paper Eater and Leo the Paper Eater. The grounds around these two were always spotless.

The south side of the midway included a basketball game, Pokerino, the Dodgem, and the old Shooting Gallery. During the 1960s, .22 caliber rifles were replaced with compressed-air machine guns from the Feltman Company of Coney Island, New York.

Ben Schiff, who pioneered the Wild Mouse ride, also marketed a new Giant Slide. Similar to slides of the early 1900s, the Giant Slide was fairly inexpensive, required little maintenance, and could be operated by just one employee.

One of Hank Clark's successful ideas was the Hawaiian Luau, offered for group picnics during the 1960s. Several Akron tire companies and the Babcock and Wilcox Company were among the companies that scheduled these festive events. Weather permitting, luaus were held in the picnic grove and highlighted by the arrival of a roasted pig borne by two park employees dressed in Hawaiian costumes.

Another promotion of the 1960s was the Miss American Teenager contest, which was staged in the ballroom. The winner of the Northeastern Ohio pageant and her court of runners-up posed on the stage at the conclusion of the evening.

104

A few people wait for hot dogs or hamburgers on a quiet day in Stand "A." The far end of the counter was reserved for soft drink and beer sales, while the near end sold hot foods.

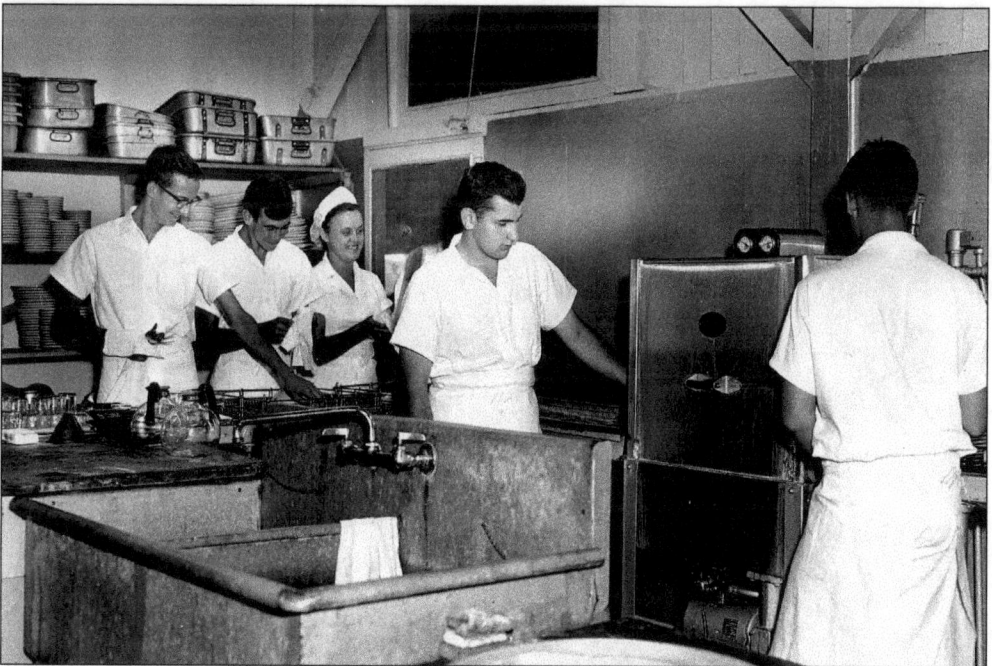

Part of the 1965 restaurant staff included Randy Hamilton, Scott Stimmel, June Farrell, Dave Francis, and Clem Kissling. Both Kissling and Francis later worked year-round at the park handling group sales and food services.

The Frozen Whip Stand, at the base of the roller coaster's main hill, was strategically located to tempt customers when entering or leaving the park. The stand offered just one flavor, vanilla, in just one size. However, three flavors of sundaes were available.

Working with a limited budget, Parker Beach modernized Chippewa during the 1960s. Improvements included a new parking admissions booth and a line of new lights on the main entrance road.

The Rocket Ship ride was antiquated by 1960s standards, but it continued to provide a cooling ride on a hot day. When the park closed in 1978, the Rocket Ship was one of only a handful of its kind still operating.

Games concessionaire Phil Jacobs removed the old miniature golf course and installed an entirely new, modern course during the early 1960s. Jacobs ran all of the park's games and held an annual Labor Day auction of left-over games prizes and house wares.

The center of the main pavilion housed the souvenir stand and picnic headquarters, which was equipped with a park-wide public address system for the use of picnic committees. The alley on the right is the service entrance to the restaurant and Stand "B."

At the south end of the main pavilion were three of Phil Jacobs' games operations, Ring Toss, Fascination, and Skee Ball. Fascination was the only air-conditioned facility in the park and was usually the most profitable of the midway games.

Charles "Dinny" Huth, whose father built the park's first penny arcade, continued to operate Chippewa's arcade until the park closed in 1978. Huth added new arcade games each season, but maintained a few of the sentimental old games that his father had manufactured during the 1920s.

Chippewa's annual July 4th parade was the envy of the amusement park industry. One entrant in the 1964 parade portrayed the popular television show, *The Beverly Hillbillies*.

Another 1964 parade participant was the Budweiser Clydesdale horse team and beer wagon. By this time, the parade was so well known that some entrants came from as far away as Canada.

The United States Air Force took advantage of the large crowds at Chippewa by staging missile displays during the 1964 season. During the Teen Fairs of the late 1960s, all of the Armed Forces placed recruiting booths in the Main Pavilion.

After operating the Oaks Hotel for more than a decade, the park sold the picturesque facility to Don Casper and Al Hutchins. The new owners closed the hotel operation and opened the Oaks Lodge, a fine dining establishment with a spectacular view of the sun setting over Chippewa Lake.

Under Parker Beach's management, the park was always freshly painted and adorned with colorful plants and well manicured lawns. While rides like the Tumble Bug were already more than 40 years old, they were maintained well and safely operated.

Although Parker Beach did not have the resources to purchase major new rides, he did contract with carnival companies to install and operate rides at the park for a single season. The Skyliner, a ski-lift type ride, was located between the ballroom and the parking lot for one season.

More exciting than the Skyliner was the fast and noisy Himalaya. Equipped with a blaring music system, the Himalaya was a big hit with teenagers, but understandably, not with local cottage owners.

112

Except when the engine of *Dynamite* roared, the pier provided a tranquil refuge from the noisy midway on summer evenings. In this 1969 photo, *Miss Chippewa* has made her last cruise of the day and was docked for the night on the inside of the L-shaped pier.

The pier was far less tranquil after a major storm of July 4, 1969, dumped eight inches of rain on the park. Eleven trees were uprooted, a portion of the midway was flooded, and the park remained closed for several days until waters receded.

After 32 seasons as owner, Parker Beach sold Chippewa Lake Park to Continental Business Enterprises Incorporated when the 1969 season ended. Admitting that the era of the family-owned amusement park was at an end, Beach retired to raise quarter horses and eventually moved to Naples, Florida, where he died in 1992.

Five

CHIPPEWA'S FINAL YEARS

Chippewa's new owner wanted to construct a year-round resort hotel that would be built north of the park. Plans for the 45-acre facility included boating, winter tobogganing, an observation tower, sports center, indoor and outdoor pools, lounges, restaurants, gift shops, a beach, and 150 guest rooms. A Ramada Inn franchise was obtained, but public resistance led to cancellation of the $6,000,000 project.

Miss Chippewa, now in poor condition, was dismantled and burned. To take her place, the steel cruise boat *Tom Sawyer* was hauled to the park from Cleveland. Unfortunately, her lack of an effective keel and her water jet propulsion made her difficult to handle on wind-swept Chippewa Lake.

The old miniature train, unused since 1962, was moved to the picnic grove and placed near a full-sized caboose and fiberglass mountain. Plans to give skiing lessons on the mountain never materialized.

116

Robert McKay, previously manager of Buckeye Lake Park and assistant general manager of Cedar Point, came to Chippewa as park manager in 1970. Under his direction, older rides were renovated, new rides were installed, and a new admissions building was constructed.

The old Spill the Milk game was operated for a few more seasons and then razed to make room for a new Round Up ride. The roller coaster (left) was thoroughly inspected and more than $40,000 was spent on new lumber. The trains were rebuilt and given a new color scheme.

The last "name" Big Band played at Chippewa in 1969. However, dance bands, rock bands, and polka bands appeared in the ballroom during the 1979s. Paul Burton's band, long famous at Cleveland's Aragon Ballroom, became Chippewa's house band and played every Saturday night during summer.

In September of 1976, the Cleveland Republican Picnic brought vice presidential candidate Robert Dole to the park as keynote speaker. Dole attracted a huge crowd but, unfortunately, just one day could not save a season in which the park lost $90,610.

In 1974, the park began a series of beauty pageants promoted by legendary talent agent, Syd Friedman of Cleveland. The events garnered a great deal of publicity, but failed to attract crowds.

Two contestants in the Miss World Pageant of July 6, 1974, posed on the miniature golf course for publicity photos. In addition to beauty pageants, Friedman also staged a Little Rascals revival production in the ballroom.

In 1976, the park was painted and decorated in celebration of the nation's bicentennial. Two years later, the park planned a series of events, including an anniversary ball, to commemorate Chippewa's centennial.

Prior to the 1977 season, the park began a major effort to renovate and modernize many of the buildings. Rustic façades, covered in wooden shingles, were installed on the Main Pavilion, and new restrooms were built at the south end of the pavilion.

The Skee Ball game's new façade gave it a fresh, pleasing appearance. The master plan for Chippewa included renovations to existing buildings and construction of new buildings designed to blend in with Chippewa's natural beauty. Hence, earth tones and forest green dominated the new color scheme.

Park employees spent the winter of 1976–77 razing old games buildings on the south side of the midway. Plans called for an expansion of the midway that would eventually connect the old midway with the Wild Mouse, Scrambler ride, and activities building erected at the southern border of the park.

The park purchased a new Scrambler ride from the Eli Bridge Company in 1977 and installed it near the border between the park and Gloria Glens Village. Other new rides included the Wild Mouse, Paratrooper, Trabant, Round-Up, and an Allan Herschell Kiddie Roller Coaster.

After razing the old games buildings and numerous cottages, the park staff began installing a new Kiddieland south of the Dodgem building and near the roller coaster. While a few of the old Kiddieland rides were used, most were newly purchased.

A new electric train replaced the old gasoline-powered train that circled the rides in the original Kiddieland. In the background is a new Paratrooper ride, and on the right is the frame of the Flying Cages.

By late April 1977, crews were rushing to complete the new Kiddieland by the second weekend in May when picnic bookings began. Traditionally, Kiddieland did not operate on the first Saturday in May, WHLO Appreciation Day.

Unlike the old Kiddieland, the new facility was pleasantly shaded on hot summer days. Kiddieland and other new rides were partly responsible for a 48 percent increase in attendance during the 1977 season. As a result, the park's losses in 1977 fell to $58,497, making it the best season since 1974.

Chippewa Lake Park reported gross revenues of $429,226 in 1977, although $99,897 of that figure was income from concessionaires. Unfortunately, operating expenses amounted to $313,161, and employee costs reached $79,160. Clearly, Chippewa could not find a way to operate at a profit.

The Original Hamburger Factory

Jim McCreedy, an experienced Ohio State Fair concessionaire, took over the games and food operations in 1978. Seeing the potential in Chippewa's future, McCreedy converted Stand "A" into the Original Hamburger Factory and gave the old stand a new look.

McCreedy also began the renovation of the restaurant, introduced new food lines, and initiated a buffet on Mother's Day, 1978. The restaurant plans, however, were never completed.

Borden's Old Fashioned Ice Cream
Chippewa Lake Park.

When Kiddieland moved from the center of the midway, McCreedy converted the area into Borden's Old Fashioned Ice Cream Plaza. Hand-dipped ice cream was served on Chippewa's midway for the first time during the 1978 season.

Next to the Maintenance Shop, McCreedy placed a portable stand called Fancy Treats that served popcorn, Sno Cones, cotton candy, and candy apples. McCreedy's improvements did a great deal to upgrade the color and appearance of the park's midway.

126

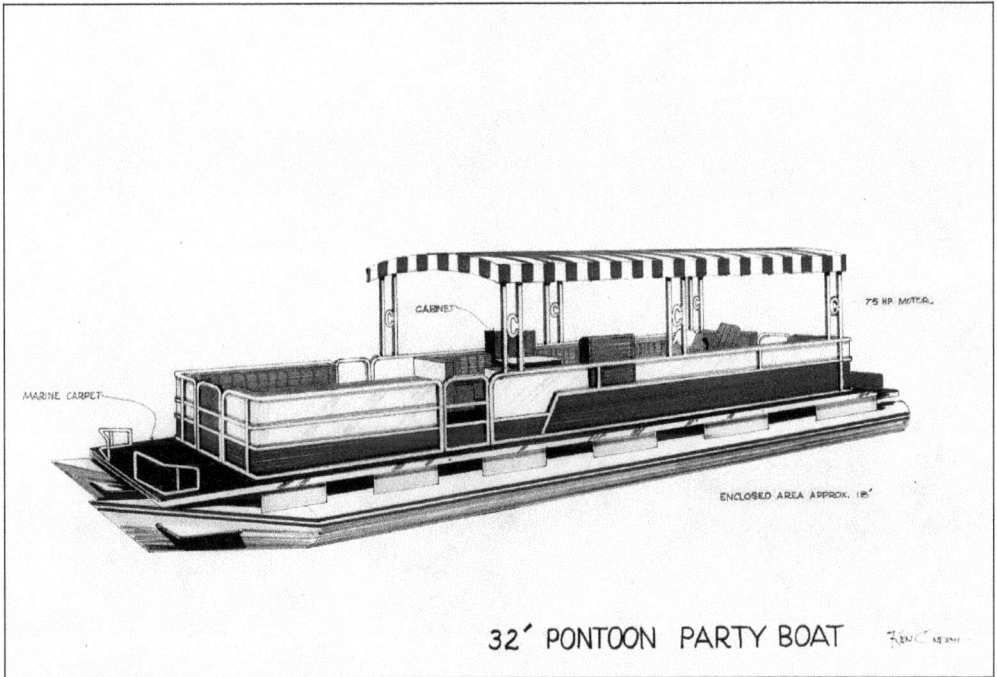

32´ PONTOON PARTY BOAT

Plans for the 1979 season called for a 32-foot boat that could be rented for parties. Although alcoholic beverages could not be served, the park planned to include food and soft drinks on cruises.

Also on the drawing board for 1979 was a complete redesign of the park's Tilt-A-Whirl ride. The redecorated ride was intended to bring color, sound, and excitement to the center of the midway.

The 1978 season was an improvement over the 1977 season. Even so, insurance, operating expenses, salaries, and declining depreciation, meant still another losing season. Late in August 1978, the park's officers regretfully decided that the park could not survive, and Chippewa Lake Park closed forever.

Carousel horses and many of Chippewa's rides were sold after the park closed. Buildings and rides that remained eventually fell prey to vandals and arsonists. Ultimately, the Main Pavilion, Hotel Chippewa, and the Ballroom were destroyed by fire. In 2004, the roller coaster and vestiges of the old midway still stood as ghostly reminders of fun-filled days and nights at Chippewa.

Visit us at
arcadiapublishing.com

www.ingramcontent.com/pod-product-compliance
Lightning Source LLC
Chambersburg PA
CBHW050652150426
42813CB00055B/1476